FARM ANIMALS

FARM DOGS

by Kathryn Clay

Consulting Editor: Gail Saunders-Smith, PhD

Consultant: Dr. Celina Johnson, College of Agriculture
California State University, Chico

CAPSTONE PRESS
a capstone imprint

Pebble Plus is published by Capstone Press,
1710 Roe Crest Drive, North Mankato, Minnesota 56003.
www.capstonepub.com

Library of Congress Cataloging-in-Publication Data
Clay, Kathryn.
Farm dogs / by Kathryn Clay.
p. cm.—(Pebble plus. farm animals)
Includes bibliographical references and index.
Summary: "Simple text and full-color photographs provide a brief introduction to farm dogs"—Provided by publisher.
ISBN 978-1-4296-8651-8 (library binding)
ISBN 978-1-62065-300-5 (ebook PDF)
1. Sheep dogs—Juvenile literature. 2. Herding dogs—Juvenile literature. 3. Cattle dogs—Juvenile literature. 4.
Livestock protection dogs—Juvenile literature. I. Title.
SF428.6.C53 2013
636.737—dc23

2011049861

Editorial Credits

Erika L. Shores, editor; Ashlee Suker, designer; Marcie Spence, media researcher; Eric Manske, production specialist

Photo Credits

Alamy: inga spence, 15; Fiona Green Animal Photography, 7; Getty Images: Jeffrey L. Jaquish ZingPix.com, 13;
iStockphoto: dageldog, 5, happyborder, cover, 1, Jan-Otto, 19, Photomorphic, 11, ShashaFoxWalters, 21; Shutterstock:
djgis, design element, Joy Brown, 17, yuris, 9

Note to Parents and Teachers

The Farm Animals series supports national science standards related to life science. This
book describes and illustrates farm dogs. The images support early readers in understanding
the text. The repetition of words and phrases helps early readers learn new words. This book
also introduces early readers to subject-specific vocabulary words, which are defined in the
Glossary section. Early readers may need assistance to read some words and to use the Table of
Contents, Glossary, Read More, Internet Sites, and Index sections of the book.

Printed in the United States of America in North Mankato, Minnesota.
042013   007246R

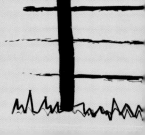

Table of Contents

Meet the Farm Dogs

Woof! Woof!

There's no time to rest.

Dogs have many jobs

around the farm.

Most farm dogs are large breeds.

They can weigh 80 pounds

(36 kilograms) or more.

Shepherds, collies, and terriers

make good farm dogs.

But many farm dogs are

a mix of more than one breed.

They are called mutts.

On the Farm

Border collies herd sheep.

The dogs guide the grazing flock

back to the barn.

An Australian cattle dog moves

cows across pastures.

The dog nips the heels

of slower cows.

A Great Pyrenees guards
the farm. It keeps coyotes
from killing chickens.

Rats and mice can scare horses
and get into grain bins.
A terrier chases the rodents
out of the barn.

Caring for Farm Dogs

Farm dogs should see a veterinarian yearly. Dogs need vaccinations against diseases such as rabies. Rabies can be spread through a bite from a skunk or a raccoon.

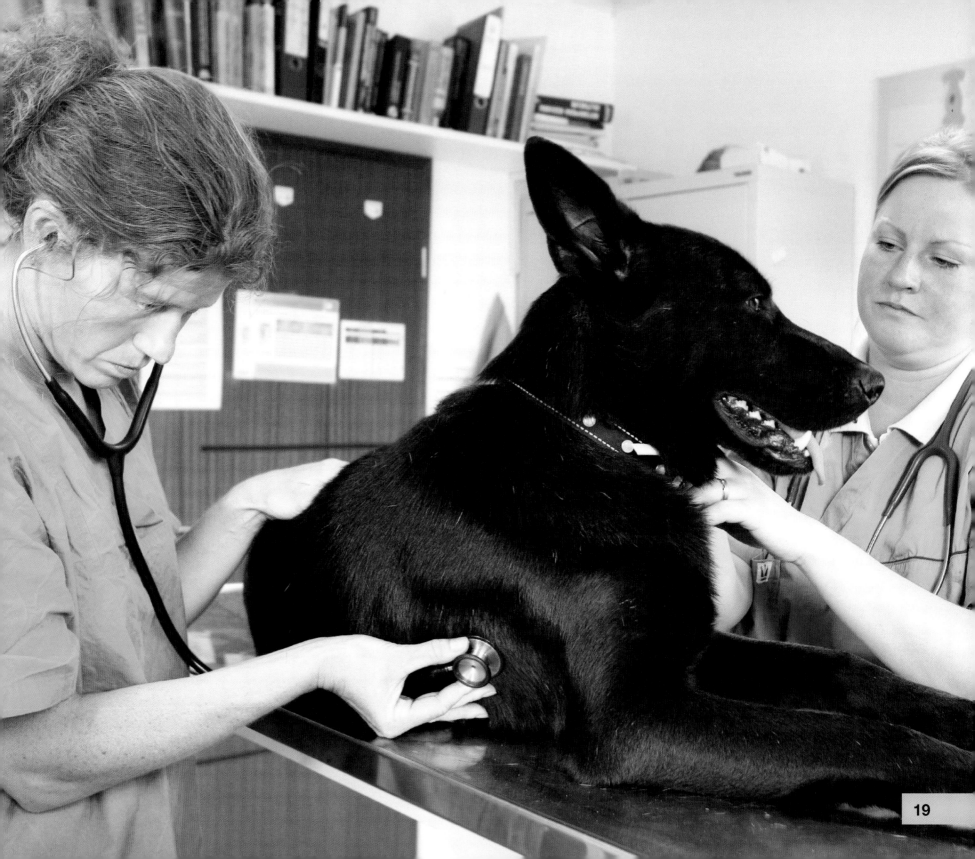

Time to Rest

It's been a long day

on the farm. Tired dogs

rest in the barn.

Some dogs sleep inside

the farmhouse with their owners.

Glossary

breed—a certain kind of animal within an animal group

collie—a breed of large dog with a long nose, a narrow head, and a thick coat

flock—a group of the same kind of animal; members of flocks live, travel, and eat together

grain bin—a large container that stores grain such as corn, wheat, or oats

herd—to bring together into a large group

pasture—land where farm animals eat grass and exercise

rabies—a deadly disease that people and animals can get from the bite of an infected animal

terrier—any of several breeds of small, lively dogs that were first bred for hunting small animals that live in burrows

vaccination—a shot of medicine that protects animals from a disease

Read More

Endres, Hollie J. *Dogs*. Farm Animals. Minneapolis: Bellwether Media, 2008.

Katz, Jon. *Meet the Dogs of Bedlam Farm*. New York: H. Holt, 2011.

Minden, Cecilia. *Farm Animals: Dogs*. 21st Century Junior Library. Ann Arbor, Mich.: Cherry Lake Pub., 2010.

Internet Sites

FactHound offers a safe, fun way to find Internet sites related to this book. All of the sites on FactHound have been researched by our staff.

Here's all you do:

Visit *www.facthound.com*

Type in this code: 9781429686518

Super-cool stuff! Check out projects, games and lots more at **www.capstonekids.com**

Index

Word Count: 166
Grade: 1
Early-Intervention Level: 17